WINTER

STARS

Winter Stars

Larry Levis

University of Pittsburgh Press

Published by the University of Pittsburgh Press, Pittsburgh, Pa., 15260
Copyright © 1985, Larry Levis
All rights reserved
Feffer and Simons, Inc., London
Manufactured in the United States of America

Library of Congress Cataloging in Publication Data

Levis, Larry.
  Winter stars.

  (Pitt poetry series)
  I. Title. II. Series.
  PS3562.E922W5 1985   811'.54   84-21957
  ISBN 0-8229-3511-2
  ISBN 0-8229-5368-4 (pbk.)

"After the Blue Note Closes," "Family Romance," "My Story in a Late Style
of Fire," "Oklahoma," "South," "There Are Two Worlds," "Two Variations on
a Theme by Kobayashi," and "Winter Stars" originally appeared in *The
American Poetry Review*. The longish poem which comprises the entire section
"Puyé," entitled "A Letter," was first published in *Antaeus*. "Adolescence,"
"The Cry," "Irish Music," and "Though His Name Is Infinite, My Father Is
Asleep" are reprinted from *Antioch Review*. "Decrescendo" and "The Quilt"
were originally published in *Quarterly West*. "Some Grass along a Ditch Bank"
first appeared in *Seattle Review*. "Whitman:" was first published in an anthol-
ogy, *Walt Whitman: The Measure of His Song* (Holy Cow! Press, 1982), and
was later reprinted in *The Pushcart Prize, VII: Best of the Small Presses*. I
would like to thank the editors of the above publications for first printing my
work.

I am especially grateful to the John Simon Guggenheim Memorial Foundation
for a fellowship which enabled me to finish the manuscript of this book of
poems.

I would like to thank Marcia Southwick, Philip Levine, and David St. John
for their constant help and understanding.

*The publication of this book is supported by grants
from the National Endowment for the Arts
in Washington, D.C., a Federal agency,
and the Pennsylvania Council on the Arts.*

For my mother and in memory of my father

CONTENTS

Winter Stars

THE POET AT SEVENTEEN

My youth? I hear it mostly in the long, volleying
Echoes of billiards in the pool halls where
I spent it all, extravagantly, believing
My delicate touch on a cue would last for years.

Outside the vineyards vanished under rain,
And the trees held still or seemed to hold their breath
When the men I worked with, pruning orchards, sang
Their lost songs: *Amapola; La Paloma;*

Jalisco, No Te Rajes—the corny tunes
Their sons would just as soon forget, at recess,
Where they lounged apart in small groups of their own.
Still, even when they laughed, they laughed in Spanish.

I hated high school then, & on weekends drove
A tractor through the widowed fields. It was so boring
I memorized poems above the engine's monotone.
Sometimes whole days slipped past without my noticing,

And birds of all kinds flew in front of me then.
I learned to tell them apart by their empty squabblings,
The slightest change in plumage, or the inflection
Of a call. And why not admit it? I was happy

Then. I believed in no one. I had the kind
Of solitude the world usually allows
Only to kings & criminals who are extinct,
Who disdain this world, & who rot, corrupt & shallow

As fields I disced: I turned up the same gray
Earth for years. Still, the land made a glum raisin
Each autumn, & made that little hell of days—
The vines must have seemed like cages to the Mexicans

Who were paid seven cents a tray for the grapes
They picked. Inside the vines it was hot, & spiders
Strummed their emptiness. Black Widow, Daddy Longlegs.
The vine canes whipped our faces. None of us cared.

And the girls I tried to talk to after class
Sailed by, then each night lay enthroned in my bed,
With nothing on but the jewels of their embarrassment.
Eyes, lips, dreams. No one. The sky & the road.

A life like that? It seemed to go on forever—
Reading poems in school, then driving a stuttering tractor
Warm afternoons, then billiards on blue October
Nights. The thick stars. But mostly now I remember

The trees, wearing their mysterious yellow sullenness
Like party dresses. And parties I didn't attend.
And then the first ice hung like spider lattices
Or the embroideries of Great Aunt No One,

And then the first dark entering the trees—
And inside, the adults with their cocktails before dinner,
The way they always seemed afraid of something,
And sat so rigidly, although the land was theirs.

ADOLESCENCE

—for Sharon and Earl

Our babysitter lives across from the Dodge Street cemetery,
And behind her broad, untroubled face.
Her sons play touch football all afternoon
Among the graves of clerks & Norwegian settlers.
At night, these huge trees, rooted in such quiet,
Arch over the tombstones as if in exultation,
As if they inhaled starlight.
Their limbs reach
Toward each other & their roots must touch the dead.

When I was fifteen,
There was a girl who loved me; whom I did not love, & she
Died, that year, of spinal meningitis. By then she
Had already left home, & was working in a carnival—
One of those booths where you are supposed
To toss a dime onto a small dish. Finally,
In Laredo, Texas, someone anonymous, & too late, bought her
A bus ticket back. . . .
Her father, a gambler & horse dealer, wept
Openly the day she was buried. I remember looking off
In embarrassment at the woods behind his house.
The woods were gray, vagrant, the color of smoke
Or sky. I remember thinking then that
If I had loved her, or even slept with her once,
She might still be alive.
And if, instead, we had gone away together
On two bay horses that farted when they began to gallop,
And if, later, we had let them
Graze at their leisure on the small tufts of spring grass
In those woods, & if the disintegrating print of the ferns
Had been a lullaby there against the dry stones & the trunks
Of fallen trees, then maybe nothing would have happened. . . .
There are times, hiking with my wife past
Abandoned orchards of freckled apples & patches of sunlight

5

In New Hampshire, or holding her closely against me at night
Until she sleeps, when nothing else matters, when
The trees shine without meaning more than they are, in moonlight,
And when it seems possible to disappear wholly into someone
Else, as into a wish on a birthday, the candles trembling . . .

Maybe nothing would have happened, but I heard that
Her father died, a year later, in a Sierra lumber camp.
He had been drinking steadily all week,
And was dealing cards
When the muscle of his own heart
Kicked him back into his chair so hard its wood snapped.
He must have thought there was something
Suddenly very young inside his body,
If he had time to think. . . .
And if death is an adolescent, closing his eyes to the music
On the radio of that passing car,
I think he does not know his own strength.
If I stand here long enough in this stillness I can feel
His silence involve, somehow, the silence of these trees,
The sky, the little squawking toy my son lost
When it slipped into the river today. . . .
Today, I am thirty-four years old. I know
That horse dealer with a limp loved his plain, & crazy daughter.
I know, also, that it did no good.
Soon, the snows will come again & cover that place
Where he sat at a wobbling card table underneath
A Ponderosa pine, & cover
Even the three cards he dropped there, three silent diamonds,
And cover everything in the Sierras, & make my meaning plain.

THE CRY

Then, everything slept.
The sky & the fields slept all the way to the Pacific,
And the houses slept.
The orchards blackened in their sleep,
And, outside my window, the aging Palomino slept
Standing up in the moonlight, with one rear hoof slightly cocked,
And the moonlight slept.
The white dust slept between the rows of vines,
And the quail slept perfectly, like untouched triangles.
The hawk slept alone, apart from this world.
In the distance I could see the faint glow
Of Parlier—even its name a lullaby,
Where the little bars slept with only one light on,
And the prostitutes slept, as always,
With the small-time businessmen, their hair smelling of pomade,
Who did not dream.
Dice slept in the hands of the town's one gambler, & outside
His window, the brown grass slept,
And beyond that, in a low stand of trees, ashes slept
Where men with no money had built a fire, and had lain down,
Beside the river,
And saw in their sleep how the cold shape of fire
Made, from each crystal of ash, the gray morning,
Which consoled no one.
Beside me, my brother slept
With a small frown knitted into his face, as if
He listened for something, his mouth open.
But there was nothing.
On my last night as a child, that sleep was final.

Above me, the shingles slept on the roof,
And the brick chimney, with smoke rising through it, slept,
And the notes on sheet music slept.
I went downstairs, then, to the room
Where my mother & father slept with nothing on, & the pale light
Shone through the window on the candor
Of their bodies strewn over the sheets, & those bodies
Were not beautiful, like distant cities.
They were real bodies
With bruises & lattices of fatigue over their white stomachs,
And over their faces.
His hair was black, & thinning. Hers was the color of ashes.
I could see every detail that disappointment had sketched,
Idly, into them: her breasts & the widening thigh
That mocked my mother with the intricate,
Sorrowing spasm of birth;
I could see
The stooped shoulders & sunken chest of my father,
Sullen as the shape of a hawk in wet weather,
The same shape it takes in its death,
When you hold it in your outstretched hand,
And wonder how it can shrink to so small a thing,
And then you are almost afraid, judging by the truculence
Of its beak & the vast, intricate plan
Of its color & delicate shading, black & red & white,
That it is only sleeping,
Only pretending a death.
But both of them really unlike anything else
Unless you thought, as I did,

Of the shape of beaten snow, & absence, & a sleep
Without laughter.
They lay there on their bed.
I saw every detail, & as I turned away
Those bodies moved slightly in the languor of sleep,
And my mother cried out once, but did not awaken,
And that cry stayed on in the air—
And even as I turned away, their frail bodies,
Seen as if for a last time,
Reminded me of ravines on either side of the road,
When I ran,
And did not know why.

WINTER STARS

My father once broke a man's hand
Over the exhaust pipe of a John Deere tractor. The man,
Rubén Vásquez, wanted to kill his own father
With a sharpened fruit knife, & he held
The curved tip of it, lightly, between his first
Two fingers, so it could slash
Horizontally, & with surprising grace,
Across a throat. It was like a glinting beak in a hand,
And, for a moment, the light held still
On those vines. When it was over,
My father simply went in & ate lunch, & then, as always,
Lay alone in the dark, listening to music.
He never mentioned it.

I never understood how anyone could risk his life,
Then listen to Vivaldi.

Sometimes, I go out into this yard at night,
And stare through the wet branches of an oak
In winter, & realize I am looking at the stars
Again. A thin haze of them, shining
And persisting.

It used to make me feel lighter, looking up at them.
In California, that light was closer.
In a California no one will ever see again,
My father is beginning to die. Something
Inside him is slowly taking back
Every word it ever gave him.
Now, if we try to talk, I watch my father
Search for a lost syllable as if it might
Solve everything, & though he can't remember, now,
The word for it, he is ashamed. . . .
If you can think of the mind as a place continually

Visited, a whole city placed behind
The eyes, & shining, I can imagine, now, its end—
As when the lights go off, one by one,
In a hotel at night, until at last
All of the travelers will be asleep, or until
Even the thin glow from the lobby is a kind
Of sleep; & while the woman behind the desk
Is applying more lacquer to her nails,
You can almost believe that the elevator,
As it ascends, must open upon starlight.

I stand out on the street, & do not go in.
That was our agreement, at my birth.

And for years I believed
That what went unsaid between us became empty,
And pure, like starlight, & that it persisted.

I got it all wrong.
I wound up believing in words the way a scientist
Believes in carbon, after death.

Tonight, I'm talking to you, father, although
It is quiet here in the Midwest, where a small wind,
The size of a wrist, wakes the cold again—
Which may be all that's left of you & me.

When I left home at seventeen, I left for good.

That pale haze of stars goes on & on,
Like laughter that has found a final, silent shape
On a black sky. It means everything
It cannot say. Look, it's empty out there, & cold.
Cold enough to reconcile
Even a father, even a son.

11

SOUTH

—for Matthew Graham

I will begin with this moth,
Its tan wings as unchanging
As the palm fronds that must still
Hang above the room I slept
In as a child, through the late,
Decaying sun of summer
Afternoons. I will focus
All my attention, now, on
The four round & delicate
Spots on each of these stiff wings—
Insignias darker than
Coffee, & I will not think
Of the way something dark, &
Utterly simple, this cup
Of coffee, trembles & then
Goes still a moment as I
Hold it, & stare past it now
A long time until I am
Remembering that woman—
How still she was the last night
We slept together—that house
We'd entered with the sudden
Giving of a door after
A year away, & a sense,
Overwhelming as the smell
Of dusk mixed with rain, that it
Belonged to no one, or rain—
The fields stretching away
On all sides of it, & those
Sparse, still trees, cottonwoods, in
The distance. And except for
A slight shuddering of hips

That said good-bye before we
Should have said anything, she
Was too knowing to talk, &,
After we had sighed, dressed, &
Turned carefully away from
Each other forever, she
Looked out a window, her face
Tilted slightly as if held
There by the quiet lights from
A town. Like light, she desired
Nothing. Sometimes, when I can
Imagine myself as that
Woman, I feel beautiful
For a moment, &, if that
Beauty continues, afraid.
It does no good to know that,
At eighteen, I was afraid
Of everything. That other
Fear is different. And what-
ever else I left, I left
Her at eighteen, naive, free,
Riding the old Norfolk &
Western through Virginia
And Kentucky, & it was
Not even painful. I sat
In the dining car before
A crystal pitcher of ice
Water & a vase full of
Marigolds & daisies &
Watched the flowers & water
Tremble as the train went on
Slowly over bridges, &

A black porter passed, a fine
Sweat already beading his
Upper lip & forehead as
He moved, serene as habit,
A small brass gong in his hand.
And whatever youth I had—
Whatever went out of me
In a fake laughter as I
Sat alone, hearing all its
Hollowness on that train—did
Not come back in the one raw
Breath dreamed, & drawn in slowly
A moment later, the first
Changed breath of a man. And I
Have not seen that boy I once
Was, gasping over what he
Thought was only a girl's final
Nakedness, unless he is
Here, in the form of this moth
On a dark sill—the design
On its wings not wallpaper
In the room where we did not
Sleep, but more intricately
Conceived, a lost design whose
Silence & austere moons might
Stand for anything now gone:

★

I think of that train ride past
Shacks, past plantation houses
White but aging in the sun
With one or two broken columns,
Stationary yet falling

14

Against the tough, undying,
Green adolescence of what
Looked like a jungled growth of
Willows, hickories, & ravines
Darkening as I glanced down;
Past junkyards embracing swamps;
Past towns so poor they were not
There, except for some grief that
Made them swell a moment beside
Those tracks, only to vanish—
A few lights slipping backward—
That was my time, or no one's,
And, lost in myself as that
Train slowed, I felt my eyes look
Out & widen until they
Took in each passing station—
Widows, soldiers, a woman
In a flowered housedress with
One leg missing, all those who
Waited, & who are now like
Photographs, still, perfect,
Staring back at me with a
Vague insolence or distrust,
And not about to be changed
By books, or revolutions.
A gray tin awning kept the
Rain off their tilted faces
Then, & they had beautiful
Faces, thin or mottled by
The sudden flaring of a match
That someone held to light his
Wife's cigarette. . . . They have all

15

Disappeared into movies,
Into tract homes & armies,
Cemeteries, calendars
Yellowing in offices,
The poultry processing plants
Of the New South, where they lose
Their dignity & fingers
To dead hens & clipping shears. . . .
That train I rode is scrap iron
Or smoke lifting in the wind. . . .
The woman I had slept with
Will turn forty this August
In a factory shaded
By tin, dark maples, sky; she
Wrings the neck of a hen, &
Stares into its clear eye, &
Stares & stares at it until
She will never laugh again. . . .
My home is a speck of dust
Glimpsed suddenly in a shaft
Of sunlight, & then gone in
A lost California as
I write this out, as always,
In longhand & in black ink,
Living one block from the sea.
Maybe, if I had a choice,
I would remember no one,
But walk on the frail water
Over the floating floors of
A madhouse until time sang
Inside my blood as if to
Cast my blood on wind, & brick.

But this is my life, no one
Else's, & what I notice
This morning is only this
Moth dead from its dumb, three-day
Efforts to fly against, &
Out of, a screened-in porch
In summer, when the hard spots
On each wing are still, empty,
And look as if no one, nothing,
Could ever decipher such
Markings, or rub them away. . . .
They are a beautiful truth
Men mount behind glass, & then
Ignore, talking of trim yachts,
Taxes, a chilled white Bordeaux.
Young, I used to envy those
Men: behind their dark, polished
Limousines perfection lurked.
I thought they were born perfect.
Slowly, I began to see
Things had been arranged this way,
And finally saw that they could
Believe only in irony,
Mozart, slums, & the best schools.
Today in the news I read of
Irish soldiers starving in
The Belfast Maze, & how, at
The end of fasting, their bones,
With no muscles left to hold
Them back, could slice their skin to
Pieces as they sleep, & turn
In their sleep. They still won't eat,

17

But lie silently as glass
Shattered in houses, or small
Hawks that have fallen a long
Way, broken or frozen blind
By snow, their eyes wide open
But no longer noticing
The simplest detail, a fly,
A drop of water, the smoke
Of some passing train scrawled on
A sky that stays there, above
Any reason for a sky.

IRISH MUSIC

Now in middle age, my blood like a thief who
Got away, unslain, & the trees hung again in the grim,
Cheap embroidery of leaves, I come back to the white roads,
The intersections in their sleeves of dust,
And vines like woodwinds twisted into shapes
For playing different kinds of silence.
Just when my hearing was getting perfect, singular
As an orphan's shard of mirror, they
Change the music into something I
No longer follow.
But how like them to welcome me home this way:
The house with its doorstep finally rotted away,
And carted off for a stranger's firewood,
And yet, behind the window there,
A woman bent over a map of her childhood, but still
A real map, that shows her people's
Ireland like a bonnet for the mad on top of
Plenty of ocean.
Hunger kept those poor relations traveling until
They almost touched the sea again,
And settled.
And there have been changes, even here.
In Parlier, California,
The band in the park still plays the same song,
But with a fresher strain of hopelessness.
This, too, will pass.
That is the message, always, of its threadbare refrain,
The message, too, of what one chooses to forget
About this place: the Swedish tailgunner who,
After twenty missions in the Pacific, chopped off
His own left hand
To get back home. No one thinks of him;

Not even I believe he found another reason, maybe,
For all left hands. So memory sires
Oblivion—this settlement of sheds, & weeds,
Where the last exile which the bloodstream always sang
Comes down to a matter of a few sparrows hopping
On & off a broken rain gutter, or downspout, & behind them,
A barn set up on a hill & meant to stay there,
Ignoring the sky
With the certainty they bolted into the crossbeams—
The whole thing
Towering over the long silent
Farmer & his wife; & that still house
Where their fingers have remembered, for fifty years,
Just where to touch the bannister; & then the steps,
That, one day, led up to me. Come home,
Say the blackened, still standing chimneys, & the missing bell
Above the three-room schoolhouse—
You've inherited all there is: the ironic,
Rueful smile of a peasant who's extinct,
Who nods, understanding, too well, the traveler,
And who orders another shot of schnapps
While his wife, pregnant, angry, puts both hands
Under her chin, & waits up.

And always, I pack the car, I answer no. . . .
When my own son was next to nothing,
He, too, would wait up with us,
Awake with hands already wholly formed,
And no larger than twin question marks in the book I closed,
One day, in a meadow,
When I reached for her—above the silent town,
Above the gray, decaying smoke of the vineyards.

A stranger who saw us there might have said:
I saw two people naked on your land.
But afterward, our pulses
Already lulling & growing singular, my eyes
Closed on that hill, I saw
A playground, mothers chatting; water falling because
It was right to *be* falling, over a cliff; & the way
Time & the lights of all home towns grew still
In that tense shape of water just before it fell . . .
I watched it a long time,
And, for no reason I could name, turned away from it,
To take that frail path along a mountainside—
Then passed through alder, spruce, & stunted pine,
Stone & a cold wind,
Up to the empty summit.

FAMILY ROMANCE

"Dressed to die . . ."
—Dylan Thomas

Sister once of weeds & a dark water that held still
In ditches reflecting the odd,
Abstaining clouds that passed, & kept
Their own counsel, we
Were different, we kept our own counsel.
Outside the tool shed in the noon heat, while our father
Ground some piece of metal
That would finally fit, with grease & an hour of pushing,
The needs of the mysterious Ford tractor,
We argued out, in adolescence,
Whole systems of mathematics, ethics,
And finally agreed that *altruism,*
Whose long vowel sounded like the pigeons,
Roosting stupidly & about to be shot
In the barn, was impossible
If one was born a Catholic. The Swedish
Lutherans, whom the nuns called
"Statue smashers," the Japanese on
Neighboring farms, were, we guessed,
A little better off. . . .
When I was twelve, I used to stare at weeds
Along the road, at the way they kept trembling
Long after a car had passed;
Or at gnats in families hovering over
Some rotting peaches, & wonder why it was
I had been born a human.
Why not a weed, or a gnat?
Why not a horse, or a spider? And why an American?
I did not think that anything could choose me
To be a Larry Levis before there even *was*

A Larry Levis. It was strange, but not strange enough
To warrant some design.
                              On the outside,
The barn, with flaking paint, was still off-white.
Inside, it was always dark, all the way up
To the rafters where the pigeons moaned,
I later thought, as if in sexual complaint,
Or sexual abandon; I never found out which.
When I walked in with a 12-gauge & started shooting,
They fell, like gray fruit, at my feet—
Fat, thumping things that grew quieter
When their eyelids, a softer gray, closed,
Part of the way, at least,
And their friends or lovers flew out a kind of skylight
Cut for loading hay.
I don't know, exactly, what happened then.
Except my sister moved to Switzerland.
My brother got a job
With Colgate-Palmolive.
He was selling soap in Lodi, California.
Later, in his car, & dressed
To die, or live again, forever,
I drove to my own, first wedding.
I smelled the stale boutonniere in my lapel,
A deceased young flower.
I wondered how my brother's Buick
Could go so fast, &,
Still questioning, or catching, a last time,
An old chill from childhood,
I thought: why me, why her, & knew it wouldn't last.

Elegies

THOUGH HIS NAME IS INFINITE, MY FATHER IS ASLEEP

When my father disappeared,
He did not go into hiding.
In old age, he was infinite,
So where could he hide? No,
He went into his name,
He went into his name, & into
The way two words keep house,
Each syllable swept clean
Again when you say them;
That's how my father left,
And that's how my father went
Out of his house, forever.
Imagine a house without words,
The family speechless for once
At the kitchen table; & all night
A hard wind ruining
The mottled skin of plums
In the orchard, & no one
Lifting a finger to stop it.
But imagine no word for "house,"
Or wind in a bare place always,
And soon it will all disappear—
Brick, & stone, & wood—all three
Are wind when you can't say
"House," & know, anymore, what it is.
Say Father, then, to no one,
Or say my father was, himself,
A house, or say each word's a house,
Some lit & some abandoned.
Then go one step further,
And say a name is a home,
As remote & as intimate.

27

Say *home,* then, or say, "I'll
Never go home again," or say,
Years later, with that baffled,
Ironic smile, "I'm on my way
Home," or say, as he did not,
"I'm going into my name."
Go further; take a chance, & say
A name is infinite. Repeat all
The names you know, all
The names you've ever heard,
The living & the dead, the precise
Light snow of their syllables.
Say your own name, or say
A last name, say mine, say his,
Say a name so old & frayed
By common use it's lost
All meaning now, & sounds
Like a house being swept out,
Like wind where there's no house.
Say finally there is no way
To document this, or describe
The passing of a father, that
Faint scent of time, or how
He swore delicately, quickly
Against it without ever appearing
To hurry the ceremony of swearing.
And say, too, how you disliked
And loved him, how he stays up
All night now in two words,
How his worn out, infinite name
Outwits death when you say it.

And say finally how the things
He had to do for you
Humiliated him until
He could not get his breath, & say
How much they mattered, how
Necessary he was. And then,
Before sleep, admit, also,
That his name is nothing,
Light as three syllables,
Lighter than pain or art, lighter
Than history, & tell how two words,
That mean nothing to anyone
Else, once meant a world
To you; how sometimes, even you,
In the sweep of those syllables,
Wind, crushed bone, & ashes—
Begin to live again.

CHILDHOOD IDEOGRAM

I lay my head sideways on the desk,
My fingers interlocked under my cheekbones,,
My eyes closed. It was a three-room schoolhouse,
White, with a small bell tower, an oak tree.
From where I sat, on still days, I'd watch
The oak, the prisoner of that sky, or read
The desk carved with adults' names: Marietta
Martin, Truman Finnell, Marjorie Elm;
The wood hacked or lovingly hollowed, the flies
Settling on the obsolete & built-in inkwells.
I remember, tonight, only details, how
Mrs. Avery, now gone, was standing then
In her beige dress, its quiet, gazelle print
Still dark with lines of perspiration from
The day before; how Gracie Chin had just
Shown me how to draw, with chalk, a Chinese
Ideogram. Where did she go, white thigh
With one still freckle, lost in silk?
No one would say for sure, so that I'd know,
So that all shapes, for days after, seemed
Brushstrokes in Chinese: countries on maps
That shifted, changed colors, or disappeared:
Lithuania, Prussia, Bessarabia;
The numbers four & seven; the question mark.
That year, I ate almost nothing.
I thought my parents weren't my real parents,
I thought there'd been some terrible mistake.
At recess I would sit alone, seeing
In the print of each leaf shadow, an ideogram—
Still, indecipherable, beneath the green sound
The bell still made, even after it had faded,
When the dust-covered leaves of the oak tree
Quivered, slightly, if I looked up in time.

And my father, so distant in those days,
Where did he go, that autumn, when he chose
The chaste, faint ideogram of ash, & I had
To leave him there, white bones in a puzzle
By a plum tree, the sun rising over
The Sierras? It is not Chinese, but English—
When the past tense, when you first learn to use it
As a child, throws all the verbs in the language
Into the long, flat shade of houses you
Ride past, & into town. Your father's driving.
On winter evenings, the lights would come on earlier.
People would be shopping for Christmas. Each hand,
With the one whorl of its fingerprints, with twenty
Delicate bones inside it, reaching up
To touch some bolt of cloth, or choose a gift,
A little different from any other hand.
You know how the past tense turns a sentence dark,
But leaves names, lovers, places showing through:
Gracie Chin, my father, Lithuania;
A beige dress where dark gazelles hold still?
Outside, it's snowing, cold, & a New Year.
The trees & streets are turning white.
I always thought he would come back like this.
I always thought he wouldn't dare be seen.

Let Nothing You Dismay

IN THE CITY OF LIGHT

The last thing my father did for me
Was map a way: he died, & so
Made death possible. If he could do it, I
Will also, someday, be so honored. Once,

At night, I walked through the lit streets
Of New York, from the Gramercy Park Hotel
Up Lexington & at that hour, alone,
I stopped hearing traffic, voices, the racket

Of spring wind lifting a newspaper high
Above the lights. The streets wet,
And shining. No sounds. Once,

When I saw my son be born, I thought
How loud this world must be to him, how final.

That night, out of respect for someone missing,
I stopped listening to it.

Out of respect for someone missing,
I have to say

This isn't the whole story.
The fact is, I was still in love.
My father died, & I was still in love. I know
It's in bad taste to say it quite this way. Tell me,
How *would* you say it?

The story goes: wanting to be alone & wanting
The easy loneliness of travelers,

I said good-bye in an airport & flew west.
It happened otherwise.
And where I'd held her close to me,
My skin felt raw, & flayed.

Descending, I looked down at light lacquering fields
Of pale vines, & small towns, each
With a water tower; then the shadows of wings;
Then nothing.

My only advice is not to go away.
Or, go away. Most

Of my decisions have been wrong.

When I wake, I lift cold water
To my face. I close my eyes.

A body wishes to be held, & held, & what
Can you do about that?

Because there are faces I might never see again,
There are two things I want to remember
About light, & what it does to us.

Her bright, green eyes at an airport—how they widened
As if in disbelief;
And my father opening the gate: a lit, & silent

City.

MY STORY IN A LATE STYLE OF FIRE

Whenever I listen to Billie Holiday, I am reminded
That I, too, was once banished from New York City.
Not because of drugs or because I was interesting enough
For any wan, overworked patrolman to worry about—
His expression usually a great, gauzy spiderweb of bewilderment
Over his face—I was banished from New York City by a woman.
Sometimes, after we had stopped laughing, I would look
At her & see a cold note of sorrow or puzzlement go
Over her face as if someone else were there, behind it,
Not laughing at all. We were, I think, "in love." No, I'm sure.
If my house burned down tomorrow morning, & if I & my wife
And son stood looking on at the flames, & if, then,
Someone stepped out of the crowd of bystanders
And said to me: "Didn't you once know . . . ?" *No*. But if
One of the flames, rising up in the scherzo of fire, turned
All the windows blank with light, & if that flame could speak,
And if it said to me: "You loved her, didn't you?" I'd answer,
Hands in my pockets, "Yes." And then I'd let fire & misfortune
Overwhelm my life. Sometimes, remembering those days,
I watch a warm, dry wind bothering a whole line of elms
And maples along a street in this neighborhood until
They're all moving at once, until I feel just like them,
Trembling & in unison. None of this matters now,
But I never felt alone all that year, & if I had sorrows,
I also had laughter, the affliction of angels & children.
Which can set a whole house on fire if you'd let it. And even then

You might still laugh to see all of your belongings set you free
In one long choiring of flames that sang only to you—
Either because no one else could hear them, or because
No one else wanted to. And, mostly, because they know.
They know such music cannot last, & that it would
Tear them apart if they listened. In those days,
I was, in fact, already married, just as I am now,
Although to another woman. And that day I could have stayed
In New York. I had friends there. I could have strayed
Up Lexington Avenue, or down to Third, & caught a faint
Glistening of the sea between the buildings. But all I wanted
Was to hold her all morning, until her body was, again,
A bright field, or until we both reached some thicket
As if at the end of a lane, or at the end of all desire,
And where we could, therefore, be alone again, & make
Some dignity out of loneliness. As, mostly, people cannot do.
Billie Holiday, whose life was shorter & more humiliating
Than my own, would have understood all this, if only
Because even in her late addiction & her bloodstream's
Hallelujahs, she, too, sang often of some affair, or someone
Gone, & therefore permanent. And sometimes she sang for
Nothing, even then, & it isn't anyone's business, if she did.
That morning, when *she* asked me to leave, wearing only
That apricot tinted, fraying chemise, I wanted to stay.
But I also wanted to go, to lose her suddenly, almost
For no reason, & certainly without any explanation.
I remember looking down at a pair of singular tracks
Made in a light snow the night before, at how they were
Gradually effacing themselves beneath the tires

Of the morning traffic, & thinking that my only other choice
Was fire, ashes, abandonment, solitude. All of which happened
Anyway, & soon after, & by divorce. I know this isn't much.
But I wanted to explain this life to you, even if
I had to become, over the years, someone else to do it.
You have to think of me what you think of me. I had
To live my life, even its late, florid style. Before
You judge this, think of her. Then think of fire,
Its laughter, the music of splintering beams & glass,
The flames reaching through the second story of a house
Almost as if to—mistakenly—rescue someone who
Left you years ago. It is so American, fire. So like us.
Its desolation. And its eventual, brief triumph.

THERE ARE TWO WORLDS

Perhaps the ankle of a horse is holy.

Crossing the Mississippi at dusk, Clemens thought
Of a sequel in which Huck Finn, in old age, became
A hermit, & insane. And never wrote it.

And perhaps all that he left out is holy.

The river, anyway, became a sacrament when
He spoke of it, even though
The last ten chapters were a failure he devised

To please America, & make his lady
Happy: to buy her silk, furs, & jewels with

Hues no one in Hannibal had ever seen.

There, above the river, if
The pattern of the stars is a blueprint for a heaven
Left unfinished,

I also believe the ankle of a horse,
In the seventh furlong, is as delicate as the fine lace
Of faith, & therefore holy.

I think it was only Twain's cynicism, the smell of a river
Lingering in his nostrils forever, that kept
His humor alive to the end.

I don't know how he managed it.

I used to make love to a woman, who,
When I left, would kiss the door she held open for me,
As if instead of me, as if she already missed me.
I would stand there in the cold air, breathing it,
Amused by her charm, which was, like the scent of a river,

Provocative, the dusk & first lights along the shore.

Should I say my soul went mad for a year, &
Could not sleep? To whom should I say so?

She was gentle, & intended no harm.

If the ankle of a horse is holy, & if it fails
In the stretch & the horse goes down, &
The jockey in the bright shout of his silks
Is pitched headlong onto
The track, & maimed, & if, later, the horse is
Destroyed, & all that is holy

Is also destroyed: hundreds of bones & muscles that
Tried their best to be pure flight, a lyric
Made flesh, then

I would like to go home, please.

Even though I betrayed it, & left, even though
I might be, at such a time as I am permitted
To go back to my wife, my son—no one, or

No more than a stone in a pasture full
Of stones, full of the indifferent grasses,

(& Huck Finn insane by then & living alone)

It will be, it might be still,
A place where what can only remain holy grazes, &
Where men might, also, approach with soft halters,
And, having no alternative, lead that fast world

Home—though it is only to the closed dark of stalls,
And though the men walk ahead of the horses slightly
Afraid, & at all times in awe of their
Quickness, & how they have nothing to lose, especially

41

Now, when the first stars appear slowly enough
To be counted, & the breath of horses makes white signatures

On the air: *Last Button, No Kidding, Brief Affair*—

And the air is colder.

OKLAHOMA

Often, I used to say: I am this dust; or, I am this wind.
And young, I would accept that. The truth is, it was never the case.
I have seen enough dust & wind by now to know
I am a little breath that always goes the distance
Longing requires, & to know even this will fail.
The truth is, dear friends, we fall apart;
And for mysterious reasons, not entirely clear to us,
We choose to live alone. The truth is,

We do *not* choose, & do not fall apart. But *are* apart. She

Dresses in the dark of a New Year, &, if she had been born a
    Catholic,
She might cross herself. But she is not a Catholic.
To clothe the temple of the soul, & that music
When the last bell on the toe of the dancer stops,
She puts on a gray silk dress, a fur coat.

It is snowing in Iowa City.

In the Old World, there was always another season.
The unpicked fruit about to fall. Nursing,
The painful suckling of infants by new mothers,
And an unchecked laughter from the workingmen's bar
Among long closed streets of wharves & warehouses
With a quiet as old as habit, or the worn sky

Over all the sleeping Bibles. I suppose it was simply

Smug, & male.

★

I rise, & put on my precisely faded jeans, a black Hawaiian shirt
With ridiculous light yellow roses; & sharp-toed
Cowboy boots.
        Style, after all, is a kind of humor,
Something truly beneath contempt,

Even here, on the Southern Plains, in Oklahoma City.

Though something, beneath the armor we put on,
Is always missing, the trouble with this wind
Is that it drives the land away: These raw cuts
In the red dirt of the roadside almost speak for themselves.
Are they painful? They look as if they once were.
Someday, see for yourself, & take care when you
Do so. Look closely, but take care.
And put your arms around each other's waists so you don't
Slip through to anything truer
Than you meant to be.

The earth, for example, has often been a lie,

And the wind its rumor.

Together once, they drove all
The better people away.

AFTER THE BLUE NOTE CLOSES

Tonight, holding a stranger in my arms—
Suddenly a downpour, a late
Summer storm. I thought of you, alone or
Not alone in that distant city,
And at that hour when the punk musicians' bars,
And the carpeted bars,
With their well-coiffed, careful clientele,
Are closing—
Those strangers pairing off at last & each desiring
What little mercy the other can
Afford. That
Wasted breath of neon light a frail
Tattoo or come-on in pools
Of rain. That street. That rain.
No. *Our* street. *Our* rain. Holding her, not you,
I watched it finally
Empty, watched until the streaked,
Reddening light of dawn came back & touched
The quiet brick of empty dance halls, touched,
Behind blackened tavern windows, a girl's cast off
Blouse; touched even the pocked faces of musicians on
The posters there: *Gun Club; Millions
Of Dead Cops*—almost as if dawn light could
Hold all things, each piece
Of shattered glass, as if to somehow bless them,
Or make them whole again.
It can't, or won't.
And it is late for blessings: All night
I've held a woman who,
Tomorrow, I will not want to see again, & who,

Tomorrow, probably will feel the same
For me. And so at last the two of us
Will have something in common:
A slight embarrassment, or,
Someday in winter, passing on a street,
A quick, amused glance before
We turn away.
I don't expect much anymore; or else
That city is so far away by now it seems
Made of great light, & distance,
Even though it was, mostly, only a house
Like any other, lit at dinnertime
By human speech, the oldest of stories; something
In common. I remember now,
After scolding him,
The precise & careful way
My two-year-old son once offered me
The crust of his own bread, holding it out
So solemnly, as if it mattered, holding it
With great care.

THE QUILT

"He had stopped believing in the goodness of the world."
—Henry James, *The Portrait of a Lady*

I think it is all light at the end; I think it is air.

Those fields we drove past, turning to mud in April,
Those oaks with snow still roosting in them. Towns so small
Their entire economy suffered if a boy, late at night,
Stole the bar's only cue ball.

In one of them, you bought an old quilt, which, fraying,
Still seemed to hold the sun, especially in one
Bright corner, made from what they had available in yellow
In 1897. It reminded me of laughter, of you. And some woman
Whose faith in the goodness of the world was
Stubborn, sewed it in. "There now," she might as well
Have said, as if in answer to the snow, which was

Merciless. "There now," she seemed to say, to
Both of us. "Here's this patch of yellow. One field gone
Entirely into light. Good-bye . . ." We had become such artists

At saying good-bye; it made me wince to look at it.
Something at the edge of the mouth, something familiar
That makes the mouth turn down. An adjustment.

It made me wince to have to agree with her there, too,
To say the day itself, the fields, each thread
She had to sew in the poor light of 1897,
Were simply gifts. Because she must be dead by now, &
Anonymous, I think she had a birthmark on her cheek;
I think she disliked Woodrow Wilson & the war;
And if she outlived one dull husband, I think she
Still grew, out of spite & habit, flowers to give away.

47

If laughter is adult, an adjustment to loss,
I think she could laugh at the worst. When I think of you both,

I think of that one square of light in her quilt,
Of women, stubborn, believing in the goodness of the world.
How next year, driving past this place, which I have seen
For years, & steadily, through the worst weather, when
The black of the Amish buggies makes the snow seem whiter,
I won't even have to look up.
I will wince & agree with you both, & past the farms
Abandoned to moonlight, past one late fire burning beside
A field, the flame rising up against the night
To take its one solitary breath, even I

Will be a believer.

DECRESCENDO

If there is only one world, it is this one.

In my neighborhood, the ruby-helmeted woodpecker's line
Is all spondees, & totally formal as it tattoos
Its instinct & solitude into a high sycamore which keeps

Revising autumn until I will look out, &
Something final will be there: a branch in winter—not
Even a self-portrait. Just a thing.

Still, it is strange to live alone, to feel something
Rise up, out of the body, against all that is,
By law, falling & turning into the pointless beauty

Of calendars. Think of the one in the office closed
For forty-three summers in a novel by Faulkner, think
Of unlocking it, of ducking your head slightly
And going in. It is all pungent, & lost. Or

It is all like the doomed singers, Cooke & Redding,
Who raised their voices against the horns'
Implacable decrescendos, & knew exactly what they

Were doing, & what they were doing was dangerous.

The man on sax & the other on piano never had to argue
Their point, for their point was time itself; & all
That one wished to say, even to close friends,
One said beside that window: The trees turn; a woman
Passing on the street below turns up her collar against
The cold; &, if the music ends, the needle on the phonograph
Scrapes like someone raking leaves, briefly, across
A sidewalk, & no one alone is, particularly, special.

That is what musicians are for, to remind us of this, unless

Those singers die, one shot in a motel room
By a woman who made a mistake; & one dead
In a plane crash, an accident.

Which left a man on sax & another on piano
With no one to back up, &, hearing the news,
One sat with his horn in a basement in Palo Alto,
Letting its violence go all the way up, &
Annoying the neighbors until the police came,
And arrested him—who had, in fact, tears
In his eyes. And the other, a white studio
Musician from L.A., who went home & tried

To cleave the keyboard with his hands until
They bled, & his friends came, & called his wife,
And someone went out for bandages & more bourbon—

Hoping to fix up, a little, this world.

Puyé

A LETTER

"I wanted to be able
To bear this. I have tried to."
—Ovid, *Metamorphoses*, Book X

It's better to have a light jacket on days like this,
Than a good memory. I would like not to remember
For a while. I would like to stroll beside
The river the way the river strolls, with its
Quick insouciance, its impatience when the shoreline
Of thick trees, factories, & lit houses
Narrows suddenly, before a low spillway
And a bridge with traffic passing or stalled above
The water which, turning white, does so only
Out of necessity, & not for anyone's amusement.
It is, maybe, a hundred feet deep in the middle.
Last week, two teenagers from Chicago, because
They were in love, held hands & jumped—& were
Pulled onto a barge by men in gray rain slicks
Who risk getting maimed daily, & who, as I
Learned later, sometimes are, & for wages that
Are water. The newspaper account said the five men
Asked the kids no questions, gave them coffee,
And talked only of baseball.
                                    On days like this,
Students lie out on the riverbank, getting
Tan. They wear next to nothing, just as,
In the nineteenth century, couples & whole families
Posed here, fully dressed, & with hats on, for
The tinted photograph. In Black River Falls,
In 1870, their mill burned, & my
Ancestors held their breath, anyway, for
An Easter portrait. They look hot, uncomfortable,
And most of the men are dressed in black suits
Too small for them. If you want to know, I'm thinking
Of the widow with the wide eyes, Nona Laroche,
Who's dead now, & who, for days after the fire,

53

Could still smell smoke on her clothes. Because she
Was French, & without money then, because
She had never voted, because all she had ever wanted
Was to live outside America, outside the stiff
Clothes framed by the photograph & the river &
The pious smoke rising from each chimney,
She had packed up everything left uncharred.
In California, in a few years, she
Had taught the men to break horses so gently
They soon sold the fastest horses south
Of Sacramento. Their voices, each morning,
Soft, transparent as silk over the corrals
And the black shade cast by oak trees.
And then, years later, ten Málaga vine cuttings,
And more on the way. Four mules. Enough water.
The smell of smoke on their clothes again for weeks
As they cleared the land & burned the silver limbs
Of cottonwoods. The bonnets the women wore
To mass were a dark lace, a mystery even
To them, & a grim Latin over their skulls—
All made from the same lace used for camisoles
Which their men would undo, later at night, when there
Was plenty of laughter, & when the first wine
Made from those grapes was so bad it was
Hilarious. And did they love each other?
Some great uncle, if the dead could shrug, & they
Can't, would say: "They loved fast horses."

Sometimes I almost believe her soul looks out
Of the photograph, almost clears the sill
Of the eyes & comes near; though it does not ever
Move, it holds me while I look at it.

But even today, I can't conceive of a soul
Without seeing a woman's body. Specifically,
Yours, undoing the straps of an evening dress
In a convertible, & then lying back, your breasts
Holding that hint of dusk mixed with mint
And the emptiness of dusk. Someone put it
Crudely: to fuck is to know. If that is true,
There's a corollary: the soul is a canary sent
Into the mines. The convertible is white, & parked
Beneath the black trees shading the river,
Mile after mile. Your dress is off by now,
And when you come, both above & below me,
When you vanish into that one cry which means
Your body is no longer quite your own
And when your face looks like a face stricken
From this world, a saint's face, your eyes closing
On some final city made entirely
Of light, & only to be unmade by light
Again—at that moment I'm still watching
You—half out of reverence & half because
The scene is distant, like a landscape, & has
Nothing to do with me. Beneath the quiet
Of those trees, & that sky, I imagine
I'm simply a miner in a cave; I imagine the soul
Is something lighter than a girl's ribbon
I witnessed, one afternoon, as it fell—blue,
Tossed, withered somehow, & singular, at
A friend's wedding—& then into the river
And swirled away. Do I chip away with my hammer?
Do I, sometimes, sing or recite? Even though
I have to know, in such a darkness, all
The words by heart, I sing. And when I come,

My eyes are closed fast. I smile, under
The earth. They loved fast horses. And someone else
Will have to watch them, grazing on short tufts
Of spring grass beside the riverbank,
When we are gone, when we are light, & grass.

★

Maybe the *soul* is only a still place in the body,
The eye & not the eye,
Something both like an altar
And like a sill opening onto a distant landscape.
Often I think of the cliff dwellings at Puyé, in New Mexico—
How the Indians deserted them
Inexplicably, & long before any white man
Knew where they were.
They rise, in their failure, miles above the plain.
They say that if you go into a cave there
You can *hear* the soul, & that it sounds
Like someone singing, & like
Someone scraping away at stone, though
No one is there.
After so many years,
You & I should go there & sit & listen for a whole day,
And say nothing to each other.
Or else, following local wisdom,
We should put sharp stones in our shoes & walk
Uphill for three miles, &,
When our feet are bleeding with that kind of pain
That isn't even pain anymore,
We should go into a cave at the top of the cliffs
And then undress each other, & stand there, not touching,
And, if we want to, cry—
For that is what the stones were for,

56

Or, not cry.
And finally, when we hear it—*if* we hear it at all—
Wait until it ceases.
And then dress & descend
In opposite directions & never again look back
At each other as we did, so often,
In bus depots, airports, bars, the porches
Of small apartments on late spring nights.
Because if we never looked back we might acquire
The true indifference of the soul as it travels,
As if on foot,
Over rocks, roots, stream beds, through
The smoke of distant cities,
Until it feels as if it is floating—
A still place in the body
That does not move,
Though we do.

★

Today, I talked to those men in the boat who
Saved the two teenagers, who
Unload off the pier there, in Rock Island, Illinois,
And who live on those barges.
Already two of the youngest of them have one
Or two fingers missing.

I finally overcame my shyness enough
To ask them, & understood at once,
When they told me

About unloading
At night—how you can hear almost nothing
As the barge draws closer & closer
To the dock, & how, often, the one light required

By state law is burned out there, & how,
Out of tiredness, you might curl your hands,
Unconsciously, & out of habit, *over* the gunwales
Of the boat, just as
The older men had cautioned you not to,
And then you can almost hear, over the slipping
Of water, the soft, hollow *thunk*
Of wood on wood. That is,
You might hear it if it weren't for the pain
At that moment—how it erases almost everything else
In your life, & all sounds, until
You know you will have this one life, this river,
As long as you live—
If only
Because no one else will hire you now.

I talked to them a long time. At a certain hour
Of night, you can hear the precise fall of every
Syllable, you can hear the slipping of water,
And you think you know why the lights
On the opposite shore
Are silent, have always been silent,
And why the Peabody coal mines in this part
Of the state are all
Boarded up by now.
And no. No one, his pick or hammer fallen to one side
Like a world, is left down there.
No one. Unless he wears an eternal smile on his face,
Which is a betrayal of all other smiles.
I don't want to believe he is real, if only
Because teenagers swim nude in the quarries
Above those mines.
And yet, now that I mention him,

I think it is only right that he is there,
Somehow, & that the mines are closed.
I would like to believe
That his grin might say how much the body
Misses its only abiding guest,
Or that the eye holes in every skull
Are merely cliff dwellings abandoned for higher, &
More lasting residences;
Or that it matters, being half French
And a descendant of certain hard-headed horse traders,
Drunks, gamblers, & women with lace camisoles
Who would as soon cut
Your throat as look at you,
And who, out of some obscure gentleness,
Decided only to stare out,
Finally, from a photograph,
As if in a kind of defiance, or bewilderment.

I wish I knew,

Though, at a certain hour
Of night, the river here is so black no one
With any intelligence would try
To tell you what it means.

★

In my light jacket, I stroll beside
The water. I am just going for a little walk.
Good-bye for a while, & good-bye to my pet names
For you—Wren, Fire, Threshold—names
Which only obscured you, & good-bye to songs the miner
Sings in the dead chill of winter, as he reaches up,

Headlamp on his helmet, to chip away at a vein
Of coal. And that sound, now, is so far away—
"God Rest Ye, Merry Gentlemen"—that I can hear,
Almost, but not quite, only his chipping away
At stone, as even that becomes a silence
In the way of something much more silent: "Let
Nothing you dismay."

Variations

WHITMAN:

> "I say we had better look our nation searchingly
> in the face, like a physician diagnosing some
> deep disease." —*Democratic Vistas*

> "Look for me under your bootsoles."

On Long Island, they moved my clapboard house
Across a turnpike, & then felt so guilty they
Named a shopping center after me!

Now that I'm required reading in your high schools,
Teenagers call me a fool.
Now what I sang stops breathing.

And yet
It was only when everyone stopped believing in me
That I began to live again—
First in the thin whine of Montana fence wire,
Then in the transparent, cast-off garments hung
In the windows of the poorest families,
Then in the glad music of Charlie Parker.
At times now,
I even come back to watch you
From the eyes of a taciturn boy at Malibu.
Across the counter at the beach concession stand,
I sell you hot dogs, Pepsis, cigarettes—
My blond hair long, greasy, & swept back
In a vain old ducktail, deliciously
Out of style.
And no one notices.
Once, I even came back as *me*,
An aging homosexual who ran the Tilt-a-Whirl
At county fairs, the chilled paint on each gondola
Changing color as it picked up speed,
And a Mardi Gras tattoo on my left shoulder.
A few of you must have seen my photographs,
For when you looked back,
I thought you caught the meaning of my stare:

63

Still water,
Merciless.

A Kosmos. One of the roughs.

And Charlie Parker's grave outside Kansas City
Covered with weeds.

Leave me alone.
A father who's outlived his only child.

To find me now will cost you everything.

SOME GRASS ALONG A DITCH BANK

I don't know what happens to grass.
But it doesn't die, exactly.
It turns white, in winter, but stays there,
A few yards from the ditch,
Then comes back in March,
Turning a green that has nothing
To do with us.
Mostly, it's just yellow, or tan.
It blends in,
Swayed by the wind, maybe, but not by any emotion,
Or partisan stripe.
You can misread it, at times:
I have seen it almost appear
To fight long & well
For its right to be, & be grass, when
I tried pulling it out.
I thought I could almost sense it digging in,
Not with reproach, exactly,
But with a kind of rare tact that I miss,
Sometimes, in others.
And besides, if you really wanted it out,
You'd have to disc it under,
Standing on a shuddering Case tractor,
And staring into the distance like
Somebody with a vision
In the wrong place for visions.
With time, you'd feel silly.
And, always, it comes back:
At the end of some winter when
The sky has neither sun, nor snow,
Nor anything personal,
You'd be wary of any impulse
That seemed mostly cosmetic.

It's all a matter of taste,
And how taste changes.
Besides, in March, the fields are wet;
The trucks & machinery won't start,
And the blades of the disc won't turn,
Usually, because of the rust.
That's when you notice the grass coming back,
In some other spot, & with a different look
This time, as if it had an idea
For a peninsula, maybe, or its shape
Reclining on a map you almost
Begin to remember.
In March, my father spent hours
Just piecing together some puzzle
That might start up a tractor,
Or set the tines of a cultivator
Or spring tooth right,
And do it without paying money.
Those rows of gray earth that look "combed,"
Between each row of vines,
And run off to the horizon
As you drive past?
You could almost say
It was almost pretty.
But this place isn't France.
For years, they've made only raisins,
And a cheap, sweet wine.
And someone had to work late,
As bored as you are, probably,
But with the added headache of
Owning some piece of land
That never gave up much
Without a mute argument.

The lucky sold out to subdividers,
But this is for one who stayed,
And how, after a few years,
He even felt sympathy for grass—
Then felt *that* turn into a resentment
Which grew, finally, into
A variety of puzzled envy:
Turning a little grass under
With each acre,
And turning it under for miles,
While half his life, spent
On top of a tractor,
Went by, unnoticed, without feast days
Or celebrations—opening his mailbox
At the roadside which was incapable
Of looking any different—
More picturesque, or less common—
The rank but still blossoming weeds
Stirring a little, maybe,
As you drove past,
But then growing still again.

TWO VARIATIONS
ON A THEME BY KOBAYASHI

The year I returned to my village, the papers
And the mail, uncensored, were delivered
Faithfully, each day.
They treated me with kindness
Where I worked, & the bars, softly lighted,
Opened every night with their music.
Appointed Master of Riddles,
I felt I had stepped onto the dock of the New World,
Toting the old one (a fresh book of poems!)
On my back. Even strangers
Bought me drinks, & someone assured me that
I would be able to get any drug I wanted,
Should I desire drugs.
And when I drove to Arkansas to read
My poems, & saw the Ozarks—
Hills full of shifting, tethered mists & a flower
That turned whole meadows white
Against the anxious hint of leaves—& when
Some of my audience walked out because I read a poem
With two obscene words, I was delighted!
For in the North, obscenities are quaint.
That year, I taught one child how to hear
Hexameters in English, & she
Stopped crying about things she could do
Nothing to change. That year,
Because I play no instrument, I met
Many musicians—they spoke to me, mostly,
Of poetry, & I told them
How, if one doesn't have much time, rhyme
And a strong refrain line ought to
Govern everything—especially if one finds himself
In a republic determined to stay young

At any cost. Something new,
I reminded them, would come, even from their fatigue
After closing. Twice, my son
Came to visit me.
And I showed him two caves in Missouri.
Mark Twain, as a child, had played in one of them.
The cave, our tour guide said, was
Over one hundred million years old. My son
Loved it—even though it is lighted,
Now, throughout, & I kept wishing that the cave
Were darker, or that I was younger.
There was nothing I could do
About either, & the blonde girl
Showing it to us knew all her lines
"By heart." Almost pretty, but she looked as if
Nothing in the world could make her laugh.
She & her children will, I'm sure, inherit this earth.

My son is four, & curious.
That year, I had to explain
My father's death to him, & also
The idea of heaven, & how
One got there, physically, after death. Therefore,
I had to lie for the first time
To my son, & therefore I had to give him up
A little more.
And though my wife & I spoke of reconciliation,
The snows came down with their ancient,
Cruel jokes, & each one
Was just as funny. Just as cruel.
We both felt stronger, after hearing
Them, & I went on
Living in my decaying neighborhood with the finch,

69

The elm, the spider, & the mouse,
And, if they could speak,
Each one spoke to me of its lowly position,
Its pathetic marriage, its doomed romance, & how
Much it hated the village—
And each one had different problems, different desires!
That year, the moon looked, each dawn,
Like a jilted suitor, a boy with an ashen face,
Sitting alone in the pool hall.
My neighbors & the townspeople avoided me,
But with the respect or courtesy
One shows for something
Misunderstood, passing, perhaps dangerous
To the education of their children—
But still a fact, like the woods sloping down
Behind an abandoned row of houses
Condemned by the new highway commissioner: bird calls,
The gray smoke of a tramp's fire,
A place where the fox we surprised, once, moved
Too quickly for human description,
And too quietly.

★

". . . No,

That year, I wore black,
And a headband flecked with crimson & meant
To terrify anyone in a gang of youths
I met, often, on the road. That year, because
Of the taxes required by the Shogunite, no one
Had any money, & often
I would pause, wondering how those who truly
Had something to complain of could
Bear it any longer—

70

Those who were poor & with sick children, whose father
Pawned heirlooms meant to last a thousand years—
The cold wind swirling through each split
Matting of rushes meant to hold
Their houses together,
Their frail argument against the wind,
Their kneeling to pray in a season
Of high fever.
I do not wish to exhibit a feeling which some,
Perhaps out of political ambition
Or simple indifference,
Might consider too generous & boastful.
Many of us thought the same things,
Many of us, in our youth, had known
Such people, & have indeed wondered where
They have gone.
Towed up the river to some new town,
We would look back at them as they
Waved to us from the pier.
We thought we would live forever, then;
We did not know we were lights dancing
On black water. Soon,
We stopped writing them long letters, although
Once, we would have said
Such letters continued to be written, always,
In our hearts. But it is
No longer fashionable to say such things, the way
We once said them, before we found out
About style, & how completely
It explains us to each other.
It is as if, without knowing it, we all
Suddenly longed to be diminished: lights going out

Along a river, & a whole
Town abandoned! But sometimes,
I still think of that great dead lord,
Whom I defended, &
For whom I would slit an enemy open, from
Forehead to abdomen, when he at last
Displayed that hint of hesitation
In the body, by which
One recognizes a liar. I moved, using one stroke;
No second thoughts.
It would have been the same for him
If I had discovered, in a sudden weightlessness
In my shoulders, a laughter throughout my whole body,
The same lie in myself.
                                    "I know
There are those who think we are thieves
Interested only in profit.
I prefer to believe, with my old master,
That there are men & women in this world
For whom I would willingly give my life, &
That we, who studied in such schools,
Are the last to know
How to move gracefully
In those exact measures meant to correct
Time, which knows
Nothing of itself, nothing
Of the damage it can do,
And which it is condemned to do:
My wife is dead;
My daughter is beautiful;
The first snow has just fallen & if I am older
It is because I have looked out & noticed it.

It is because
It has tricked me into this final maneuver,
This turning toward a white window,
Something my master always told me it would do, &
Against which all swords are useless!"

THOSE GRAVES IN ROME

There are places where the eye can starve,
But not here. Here, for example, is
The Piazza Navona, & here is his narrow room
Overlooking the Steps & the crowds of sunbathing
Tourists. And here is the Protestant Cemetery
Where Keats & Joseph Severn join hands
Forever under a little shawl of grass
And where Keats' name isn't even on
His gravestone, because it is on Severn's,
And Joseph Severn's infant son is buried
Two modest, grassy steps behind them both.
But you'd have to know the story—how bedridden
Keats wanted the inscription to be
Simple, & unbearable: "Here lies one
Whose name is writ in water." On a warm day,
I stood here with my two oldest friends.
I thought, then, that the three of us would be
Indissoluble at the end, & also that
We would all die, of course. And not die.
And maybe we should have joined hands at that
Moment. We didn't. All we did was follow
A lame man in a rumpled suit who climbed
A slight incline of graves blurring into
The passing marble of other graves to visit
The vacant home of whatever is not left
Of Shelley & Trelawney. That walk uphill must
Be hard if you can't walk. At the top, the man
Wheezed for breath; sweat beaded his face,
And his wife wore a look of concern so
Habitual it seemed more like the way
Our bodies, someday, will have to wear stone.
Later that night, the three of us strolled,

74

Our arms around each other, through the Via
Del Corso & toward the Piazza di Espagna
As each street grew quieter until
Finally we heard nothing at the end
Except the occasional scrape of our own steps,
And so said good-bye. Among such friends,
Who never allowed anything, still alive,
To die, I'd almost forgotten that what
Most people leave behind them disappears.
Three days later, staying alone in a cheap
Hotel in Naples, I noticed a child's smeared
Fingerprint on a bannister. It
Had been indifferently preserved beneath
A patina of varnish applied, I guessed, after
The last war. It seemed I could almost hear
His shout, years later, on that street. But this
Is speculation, & no doubt the simplest fact
Could shame me. Perhaps the child was from
Calabria, & went back to it with
A mother who failed to find work, & perhaps
The child died there, twenty years ago,
Of malaria. It was so common then—
The children crying to the doctors for quinine,
And to the tourists, who looked like doctors, for quinine.
It was so common you did not expect an aria,
And not much on a gravestone, either—although
His name is on it, & weathered stone still wears
His name—not the way a girl might wear
The too large, faded blue workshirt of
A lover as she walks thoughtfully through
The Via Fratelli to buy bread, shrimp,

And wine for the evening meal with candles &
The laughter of her friends, & later the sweet
Enkindling of desire; but something else, something
Cut simply in stone by hand & meant to last
Because of the way a name, any name,
Is empty. And not empty. And almost enough.

Sensationalism

THE ASSIMILATION OF THE GYPSIES

In the background, a few shacks & overturned carts
And a gray sky holding the singular pallor of Lent.
And here the crowd of onlookers, though a few of them
Must be intimate with the victim,
Have been advised to keep their distance.
The young man walking alone in handcuffs that join
Each wrist in something that is not prayer, although
It is as urgent, wears
A brown tweed coat flecked with white, a white shirt
Open at the collar.
And beside him, the broad, curving tracks of a bus that
Passed earlier through the thawing mud . . . they seem
To lead him out of the photograph & toward
What I imagine is
The firing squad: a few distant cousins & neighbors
Assembled by order of the State—beside
The wall of a closed schoolhouse.
Two of the men uneasily holding rifles, a barber
And an unemployed postal clerk,
Are thinking of nothing except perhaps the first snowfall
Last year in the village, how it covered & simplified
Everything—the ruts in the road & the distant
Stubble in the fields—& of how they cannot be,
Now, any part of that. Still,
They understand well enough why
The man murdered the girl's uncle with an axe,
Just as they know why his language,
Because it was not official & had to be translated
Into Czech at the trial, failed to convince
Anyone of its passion. And if
The red-faced uncle kept threatening the girl
Until she at last succumbed under a browning hedge, & if
The young man had to use three strokes with the axe

To finish the job—well, they shrug,
All he had, that day, was an axe.
And besides, the barber & the clerk suspect that this boy,
Whom they have known for half their lives,
Had really intended to kill the girl that evening—
Never the uncle.
In a lost culture of fortune tellers, unemployable
Horse traders, & a frank beauty the world
Will not allow,
It was the time of such things, it was late summer,
And it is time now, the two executioners agree,
That all of this ended. This is
Jarabina. 1963. And if
Koudelka tells us nothing else about this scene,
I think he is right, if only because
The young man walks outside time now, & is not
So much a murderer as he is, simply, a man
About to be executed by his neighbors. . . .
And so it is important to all of them that he behave
With a certain tact & dignity as he walks
Of his own accord but with shoulders hunched,
Up to the wall of the empty schoolhouse;
And, turning his head
First to one side, then to the other,
He lets them slip the blindfold over his eyes
And secure it with an old gentleness
They have shared
Since birth. And perhaps at this moment
All three of them remember slipping light scarves,
Fashioned into halters,
Over the muzzles of horses, & the quickness of horses.
And if the boy has forgiven them in advance
By such a slight gesture, this turning of his head,

80

It is because he knows, as they do, too,
Not only that terror is a state
Of complete understanding, but also that
In a few years, this whole village, with its cockeyed
Shacks, tea leaves, promiscuity between cousins,
Idle horse thieves, & pale lilacs used
To cure the insane,
Will be gone—bulldozed away so that the land
Will lie black & fallow & without history.
And nothing will be planted there, or buried,
As the same flocks of sparrows
Will go on gathering, each spring, in the high dark
Of these trees.
Still, it is impossible not to see
That the young man has washed & combed his hair
For this last day on earth; it is impossible
Not to see how one of the policemen has turned back
To the crowd as if to prevent
Any mother or sister from rushing forward—
Although neither one, if she is here, seems
About to move. And in the background,
You can see that a few of the houses are entirely white,
Like a snowfall persisting into spring,
Or into oblivion, though this
May be the fault of the photograph or its development
Under such circumstances. . . .
And now even the children in the crowd, who have gathered
To watch all this, appear to be growing bored
With the procedures & the waiting.
I suppose that the young man's face,
Without looking up, spoke silently to Koudelka as he passed,
Just as it speaks now, to me, from this photograph.
Now that there is nothing either of us can do for him.

His hair is clean & washed, & his coat is buttoned.
Except for his handcuffs, he looks as if
He is beginning a long journey, or going out,
For the first time into the world. . . .
He must have thought he could get away with this,
Or else he must have thought he loved her.
It is too late to inquire.
It is mid-afternoon & twenty years too late,
And even the language he used to explain it all
Is dying a little more, each moment, as I write this—
And as I begin to realize that
This ancient, still blossoming English
Will also begin to die, someday, to crack & collapse
Under its own weight—
Though that will not happen for years & years,
And long after the barber & the clerk
Have lowered their rifles & turned away to vomit
For what seems like a long time, & then,
Because there is nothing else for them to do,
They will walk home together, talking softly in a language
That has never been written down.
If you look closely at the two of them
Sweating in their black wool suits,
You can see how even their daily behavior,
The way they avoid the subject,
Has become an art:
One talks of his daughter, who is learning to dance.
The other mentions his mother, who died, last year—
When the orchards were simple with their fruit,
And ripe—of an undiagnosed illness.
And if the lots they pass are empty because the horses
Were shipped off years ago to Warsaw
For the meat on their backs?

And if there is no hope for this,
Or any poetry?
On their lips the quick syllables of their
Language fly & darken into a few, last
Delicious phrases, arpeggios—
Even though they are talking of ordinary life
As they pass the smells of cooking
Which rise in smoke from the poorest of houses
And even from stoves carried outdoors & burning,
As fuel, the cheap paneling of shacks
Which the government gave them.
Until it seems that all they are
Rises in smoke,
As it always has,
And as it will continue to do in this place
For a few more years.

SENSATIONALISM

In Josef Koudelka's photograph, untitled & with no date
Given to help us with history, a man wearing
Dark clothes is squatting, his right hand raised slightly,
As if in explanation, & because he is talking,
Seriously now, to a horse that would be white except
For its markings—the darkness around its eyes, muzzle,
Legs & tail, by which it is, technically, a gray, or a dapple gray,
With a streak of pure white like heavy cream on its rump.
There is a wall behind them both, which, like most walls, has
No ideas, & nothing to make us feel comfortable. . . .
After a while, because I know so little, &
Because the muted sunlight on that wall will not change,
I begin to believe that the man's wife & children
Were shot & thrown into a ditch a week before this picture
Was taken, that this is still Czechoslovakia, & that there is
The beginning of spring in the air. That is why
The man is talking, & as clearly as he can, to a horse.
He is trying to explain these things,
While the horse, gray as those days at the end
Of winter, when days seem lost in thought, is, after all,
Only a horse. No doubt the man knows people he could talk to:
The bars are open by now, but he has chosen
To confide in this gelding, as he once did to his own small
Children, who could not, finally, understand him any better.
This afternoon, in the middle of his life & in the middle
Of this war, a man is trying to stay sane.
To stay sane he must keep talking to a horse, its blinders
On & a rough snaffle bit still in its mouth, wearing

Away the corners of its mouth, with one ear cocked forward
   to listen,
While the other ear tilts backward slightly, inattentive,
As if suddenly catching a music behind it. Of course,
I have to admit I have made all of this up, & that
It could be wrong to make up anything. Perhaps the man
   is perfectly
Happy. Perhaps Koudelka arranged all of this
And then took the picture as a way of saying
Good-bye to everyone who saw it, & perhaps Josef Koudelka was
Only two years old when the Nazis invaded Prague.
I do not wish to interfere, Reader, with your solitude—
So different from my own. In fact, I would take back everything
I've said here, if that would make you feel any better,
Unless even that retraction would amount to a milder way
Of interfering; & a way by which you might suspect me
Of some subtlety. Or mistake me for someone else, someone
Not disinterested enough in what you might think
Of this. Of the photograph. Of me.
Once, I was in love with a woman, & when I looked at her
My face altered & took on the shape of her face,
Made thin by alcohol, sorrowing, brave. And though
There was a kind of pain in her face, I felt no pain
When this happened to mine, when the bones
Of my own face seemed to change. But even this
Did not do us any good, &, one day,
She went mad, waking in tears she mistook for blood,
And feeling little else except for this concern about bleeding

Without pain. I drove her to the hospital, & then,
After a few days, she told me she had another lover. . . . So,
Walking up the street where it had been raining earlier,
Past the darkening glass of each shop window to the hotel,
I felt a sensation of peace flood my body, as if to cleanse it,
And thought it was because I had been told the truth. . . .
  But, you see,
Even that happiness became a lie, & even that was taken
From me, finally, as all lies are. . . . Later,
I realized that maybe I felt strong that night only
Because she was sick, for other reasons, & in that place.
And so began my long convalescence, & simple adulthood.
I never felt that way again, when I looked at anyone else;
I never felt my face change into any other face.
It is a difficult thing to do, & so maybe
It is just as well. That man, for instance. He was a *saboteur*.
He ended up talking to a horse, & hearing, on the street
Outside that alley, the Nazis celebrating, singing, even.
If he went mad beside that wall, I think his last question
Was whether they shot his wife & children before they threw them
Into the ditch, or after. For some reason, it mattered once,
If only to him. And before he turned into paper.

NOTES

"The Poet at Seventeen" is meant to recall Rimbaud's title. Other lines in the poem intentionally echo Pound and Baudelaire.

"The Cry" is at least partially indebted in its methods to Joseph Brodsky's poem, "Grand Elegy." The poem also borrows a phrase freely translated from the Spanish of Pablo Neruda.

"After the Blue Note Closes"—The Blue Note is a rock music bar in Columbia, Missouri.

The setting of "The Quilt" is the Amish settlement of Kalona, Iowa.

"Two Variations on a Theme by Kobayashi" is of course indebted to Kobayashi's film, *Hari Kari*. The speaker of the second half of the poem is the Samurai warrior, and central character, of the film.

Both "The Assimilation of the Gypsies" and "Sensationalism" are personal interpretations of Koudelka's photographs. Although some incidents in both poems are corroborated by historical fact, neither poem is meant to suggest that such facts are necessarily the facts of either photograph.

The poems in this book are arranged in the approximate chronological order of their writing. The book was begun in Iowa City in 1980 and finished in Bucharest in 1983.

PITT POETRY SERIES
Ed Ochester, General Editor